EAT SMART

EAT SMART

The Science of Nutrition and Longevity

JUDE HAWTHORNE

QuillQuest Publishers

CONTENTS

CHAPTER 1

Introduction

Food is where everything begins, and the old saying "an apple a day keeps the doctor away" is really quite true. A lot of folks here probably know exactly where I am coming from now. The saying "let food be thy medicine" hangs in my office. More than three decades ago, I realized the profound impact that nutrition has on health and health on nutrition. For the last 35 years, I have been practicing lifestyle medicine, in which nutrition plays a large role. After a little research on the Internet, I found that the adage "let food be thy medicine" stemmed from the 1550 B.C. Ebers Papyrus. By then, the ancient Egyptians realized that there were certain foods that could make them feel better. This has been an ongoing concept for thousands of years. We are now going to examine this concept more closely.

Eat Smart: The Science of Nutrition and Longevity is the fifth talk in a six-part lecture series from the Department of Neurology. This talk examines how foods relate to health, provides guidelines to eat smart for maximum health and longevity, and demonstrates easy food preparation techniques that make breaking the fast and eating five delicious, health-promoting meals a day a breeze. Research has shown that what we consume has a profound effect on our health. This is true from a broad perspective as well. The old adage "you are what you eat" is really quite true.

CHAPTER 2

The Basics of Nutrition

We do not, however, suggest that those are the only rules to guide daily eating. Nonetheless, they are apparent universal guides that we believe it would be good for many people to get to know about. And it is not only the common man who might be tempted to give them a fair go - the guidelines we discuss here are already found useful by a callant group of specialists in the field. Animal studies are probably much of the reason for this, and this is because they have great potential: they allow very large numbers of individuals to be treated, and they are relatively malleable in many ways. We will see how those peculiarities are put to use when these guidelines have been reformulated as the biology of specific macronutrients - in the main fatty acids, glucose, and amino acids - and their abode in a cardiac intervention named periodic fasting.

We are all different - every body is slightly unique - and our genetic profiles and life histories affect which nutrients make us feel good and on which foods we thrive. Yet, not only do we all share the same roughly 20,000 genes, but almost all of us also expect the same dietary rules to be good for us. This is a matter of perspective. It can be regarded as an example of a shared human body plan that has served the development of synthetic, apprehensible rules to steer the eating or much of mankind - guidelines on what is on our daily menu. This text is about such rules, although in a somewhat broader sense, for the rules we discuss here are mathematical ones resting on principles of physics none of us can tamper with.

CHAPTER 3

Macronutrients and Micronutrients

Proteins are polymers of amino acids, which are united by simple bonds and can be hydrolyzed. They constitute the main part of organic tissue, accounting for 20% of our body weight. Muscle tissue, in particular, has the highest protein content and plays a crucial role in various organic functions, including enzymatic, neurological, and immune functions. Proteins are also responsible for transporting oxygen from the lungs to the cells. Approximately 10% of the energy produced during catabolism comes from proteins and their constituent amino acids. It is important to maintain a balanced protein intake as it regulates and controls various cellular processes. In individuals with renal insufficiency, protein restriction is recommended as a preventive measure, rather than excessive protein intake commonly seen in high-protein diets. Athletes may need to increase their protein intake, but it should be done in moderation to avoid issues such as urinary and bone acidosis caused by excessive protein consumption.

The main components of foods in the human diet - macronutrients: water, proteins, fats, and carbohydrates - are essential for providing us with energy and essential structural components such as membranes and muscle fibers. They also play a crucial role in many cellular and bodily processes. Micronutrients, such as vitamins and minerals, are equally important as they contribute to the regulation of enzymatic processes. Although they are required in small amounts, they are fundamental for our health. Water and minerals, also known as "elements of ash" due to their low caloric content, are the main components of the tissues and cells in our body. They are largely responsible for our body weight. Water also performs various biological functions, including the transport of minerals and nutrients, the excretion of waste substances, and the regulation of body temperature.

CHAPTER 4

The Role of Carbohydrates in a Healthy Diet

Fruits, vegetables, grains, and legumes provide glucose in the form of long chains of glucose molecules known as carbohydrates. All the cells in the body use glucose to make energy to function. When cells do not have access to glucose or oxygen, it can cause tissue damage and may cause certain diseases or conditions. There are two types of carbohydrates: complex and simple carbohydrates. Simple carbohydrates include sugars such as glucose and fructose, while complex carbohydrates include polysaccharides and fiber. Every day, the body requires a certain amount of energy. The most important goal is to obtain most of these calories from complex carbohydrates and reduce the number of simple sugar calories. Whether the source of glucose is in the form of complex or simple carbohydrates, in a balanced diet, both are important and will provide the necessary energy for the body in the short, medium, and long term - always opting for a source with high dietary fiber.

Carbohydrates such as fruits, vegetables, grains, and legumes are an essential part of our diet since they provide energy in the form of glucose, which is needed by the body for the functioning of the central nervous system, kidney, muscles, and heart. Over time, after consuming a meal, the blood glucose level will drop, the pancreas will produce insulin to store the glucose in the liver and muscle as glycogen, and any excess amount in fat cells as triglycerides. When the blood glucose level drops again, the insulin level decreases, and the glucose stored in the liver as glycogen is released into the blood, raising the blood glucose level so that the body can function. The body will store glucose in the form of liver and muscle glycogen, with a maximum of about 500 grams, which can provide energy for about 12-24 hours.

CHAPTER 5

The Importance of Proteins for Longevity

As we have seen earlier, the proper amount of essential amino acids in the proteins of the diet can activate the maintenance process, which implies that the most important mechanism by which a "low"-protein diet activates the maintenance is through the optimization of the quality of the proteins of the diet. This fact has been recently demonstrated in the laboratory, where animals have been placed on a deficient protein diet and simultaneously deprived of essential amino acids. The result was evident: activation of the same mechanisms that lead to re-addressing resources from growth to maintenance and, therefore, a significant reduction in lifespan. In humans, the sources of proteins that contain optimal amounts of essential amino acids are mainly of animal origin, such as those of lean meats, fish, and eggs. However, not all proteins of animal origin are rich in essential amino acids. The processes of industrial refining and deproteinization to which proteins and other nutrients in food are normally subjected can lead to a significant loss of these important components, and therefore, it is necessary to divert attention to these practices.

Low protein intake sensed by the cell activates a series of intracellular actions that, in the end, lead to extending lifespan. On the other hand, protein in excess also activates actions within the cells, but in this case, those actions promote damage and the onset of age-related diseases. Hence, it is the result of these at the end of life or the balance between them, either of which depends directly on the levels of protein intake, that determine longevity and the length of health span. Therefore, protein intake can be seen as one of the most important features of the diet in terms of proper aging.

CHAPTER 6

The Power of Healthy Fats

Dietary fats, like carbohydrates, may come in two types. There are the good fats (monounsaturated and polyunsaturated) and the bad fats (saturated and trans). However, the upper levels of Pharaoh's plant-rich diet were packed with the former. These malleable unsaturated fatty acids enfolded in goodness supported his dynasty by driving the nearly 3,000-year-old Egyptian ruler's increasable heartbeat rate, underwriting his visits to the frenzy-plagued Pharaoh bathrooms, camp sites, and his God-fearing subjects. These healthful fats had stampeded ancient Egypt — home of the first-in-position stone monuments. They still play pivotal performs in the majestic life of the Egyptian people.

Healthy fats are an essential component of a good diet, linking with heart, brain, and overall health. In the early 1990s, scientists trained their microscopes on the global dietary epidemic. They watched as everyone in every major city embarked on a low-fat diet. After this advice was adopted, what happened is slowly emerging. Carbohydrate consumption climbed, and so did rates of obesity, diabetes, and heart disease. For the first known time, the world ceased to survive on fat — a macronutrient that supports the growth of energy-generating capabilities in every cell membrane — a layer to the body's billions of cells, which receive and supply the good things in life. Once the burden of fat becomes welcome in the body, the sum experiences a momentous and long-term shift toward health.

CHAPTER 7

Understanding Vitamins and Minerals

Iron, that will help deliver oxygen, and zinc, with the body's immune system. Found, respectively, in dark leafy greens and uses's stem protection spice, zinc is rich in these healthful foods as well as in legumes such as beans, and whole and refined grains, such as wheat, rice, and corn that helps with selective absorption. The journal of nutrition reports: well-balanced health lifestyle choices, including people's lifestyle choices, including eating food, healthy on fruits and vegetables, whole grain, plant-based diets that are contributing to oxidative stress and antioxidant defense are positively associated with cognitive functions. Among seventy-eight, older participants, and we're also linked to reduce marker inflammation.

Minerals. Important beautiful flavors that contain dietary healthful benefits, magnesium, calcium, copper, and phosphorus can help make exercise more effective positively change thinking and reduce inflammation, and shifting homeostasis in useful subdivision are so easy to find in the leafy green beautiful foods asked by the daily dozen to be included in your diet. The vitamins will help regulate water balance in the body.

One could argue with large quantities of vitamin supplements that are ingested individually or seen smaller nutrients, if the remaining supplements take over the jobs those nutrients do in combination with one another, may then work less effectively together. This may be the reason why large clinical trials of multi-vitamins have not shown lower heart disease, osteoarthritis, or cancer incidence. The research on well-balanced healthful diets no doubt includes the combined benefits of seemingly competing valuable nutrients. With that being said, popular and important studies suggest that combination of foods with nutrients can decrease inflammation and a decrease in certain nutrition-related effects changes over time.

Vitamins. Vitamin and mineral supplements should never replace a diet healthy in fruits and vegetables and other whole foods, nor the beneficial foods that contain unsaturated fats that act as antioxidants or the healthful herbs and spices that have been used in many cultures to help with digestion, to make food more fun and hopefully reduce inflammation as well. I will be asking myself about unsupplemented plant-based foods with significant combined quantities to make sure they help with bioavailability, that is, absorption, staying in our systems long enough to benefit, before entering the excretory pathway. We have evolved with these combined foods for hundreds and thousands of years.

CHAPTER 8

The Impact of Water on Nutrition and Longevity

That supplementation with water induces pathologies due to increased consumption of beverages, regardless of toxicity and fragrance, overwhelming stress resistance, diseases, and reliable results in spite of small sample sizes, to the contribution of water in further increasing mean lifespan at ad libitum level of diet are deprived of any theoretical substantiation and experimental evidence and contradict a bulk of sound and reliable data of social objective natural sciences. As any biological exposures, hydration with water could promote successful survival with milder restrictive manipulations stress, amelioration of aging, and diseases that have been noticed. If such a simple and effective method for a broad range of diet and lifespan manipulations for different inbred and outbred strains and stocks of animals existed, results of hundreds of experiments that were published in existing databases would be confidential, would have been submitted for open research, and had been positive in the absence of fraud.

Further evidence for the lack of a 'specific damage effect' during the late lifespan from late-onset hydration treatment with hot water was obtained by studies of various morphological, functional, cognitive, and some other parameters, as well as on the mean lifetime of spontaneous and actuarial aging in C57Bl/6NNia mice. It was shown that chronic treatment with hot water delayed age-related alterations and extended mean lifetime in both males and females, with more marked effects in males, in whom significant deviations from the control mean values had never appeared. The results provide support for the pro-survival geroprotective effect of chronic hyperhydration. The mechanisms of the longevity-increasing geroprotective activity of hydration effects are discussed in greater detail in the Western Reserve University Medical thesis and in Parts 9 and 10.

CHAPTER 9

The Science Behind Antioxidants

Micronutrients are a group of nutrients including vitamins, antioxidants, and trace metals such as iron, copper, zinc, and selenium. The role of these micronutrients in the biological functional activities includes that they are antioxidants, enzyme cofactors, immune-activity modulators, or other functional benefits, as well as necessary elements for metabolites' composition. Lack of these nutrients can impair cellular oxidative mitochondrial metabolism and genes' expression or promote inflammation, leading to the development of aging, chronic disease, even a short lifespan. Consequently, bodies require daily nutrition maintenance through the oral intake of food. Antioxidants are critical defense agents and our primary resources. However, no single antioxidant can act collectively to provide a complete shield. Scientists believe that it is not the quantity of antioxidants in an individual's diet that leads to longevity, but rather the variety of antioxidants. Antioxidants also help repair damaged cells. Reckon this fact: at any given moment, it is estimated that about one million working cells are damaged. Antioxidants naturally prevent this destructive activity from happening.

Eating smart may help to promote longevity and vitality and protect our bodies from sickness and disease. Current scientific discoveries, together with a great deal of evidence from history and cultures, support that optimizing what we eat is critically important. According to studies such as those from the National Institute on Aging at the National Institutes of Health, where people are living longer today than ever before, what we eat and the supplements we take to compensate for these missing micronutrients may play a significant role. Researchers have presented a compelling argument, on the basis of life-span studies from animals up to humans, as well as research in cellular senescence, the process of aging, to suggest that decreases in the rate of aging can be achieved by decreasing chronic tissue stress in many ways—one of which is to supplement cells with antioxidants.

CHAPTER 10

The Benefits of Phytochemicals

The health benefits of the phytochemicals are well-established. Regular consumption of plant-based diets has been shown to reduce the risk of chronic diseases. It is proposed that a diet high in fruits may reduce the risk of developing heart diseases and may protect against certain cancers such as oral, esophageal, lung, and bladder cancers. Much of the credit goes to the phytochemicals in fruits which also possess antioxidant properties. Those who consume plant-based diets contain high levels of the powerful group of antioxidants such as vitamins C and E, carotenoids, and flavonoids. There have been a number of intervention trials on diet and cancer risk. In the majority of studies, the risk is moderately lower for people who eat more fruits and vegetables compared to those who consume less.

Low-calorie, but bulky, fiber-rich fruits and vegetables help you feel full. This makes it easier to control calorie intake and keep body weight in check. An enriched mix of bell peppers illuminates enhanced ability to neutralize a cross-section of cancer-promoting toxins. In one test, a mix of seven phytochemicals that gave off different colored emissions in the presence of chemical toxins, including dangerous nitrosamines, neutralized different mutagens simultaneously. In some cases, it was the combination and interaction of two or more compounds working together to create the observed effect. Cruciferous vegetables, such as carrots, sweet potatoes, peas, and cauliflower, each contain a phytochemical profile that also works in different ways to reduce toxic response. This speaks to the importance of eating colorful fruits and vegetables in a balanced diet.

The best sources of phytochemicals are colorful fruits, vegetables, and whole grains. Like vitamins and minerals, they are considered essential nutrients for preventing chronic disease. Diets high in fruits, vegetables, whole grains, and legumes and lentils have been consistently linked with reduced risk of chronic diseases, such as certain cancers, heart disease, stroke, high blood pressure, diabetes, and obesity. There are a number of proposed mechanisms for the observed benefits when fruits and vegetables (in a balanced diet) are consumed. Phytochemicals have free-radical-scavenging potential and can also regulate enzymes that detoxify carcinogens.

CHAPTER 11

The Role of Fiber in a Balanced Diet

There has been, however, a longstanding debate among doctors and nutritionists over the role of dietary fiber in health. One of the big things that distinguishes eating plant-based diets from vegetarian and meat-eating diets is fiber consumption. If you eat a quarter of a cup of fruit or a few tablespoons of vegetables in comparison to a cup of fruit and between one and two and a half cups of vegetables—all in one meal—such a shift would be dramatically increasing fiber intake. A lot of people think that fiber is important only for changing bowel habits, but increased fiber intake has also been shown to benefit a number of other health parameters.

All whole plant foods, not just fruits, vegetables, nuts, and seeds, contain various important nutrients. This ties into the debate over fiber. Does fiber have any nutritional value? Metabolically, it may be considered nonessential, but it is definitely not of no overall importance to health. Fiber is the outer layer of plant cell walls. Whole plant foods, such as beans, whole grains, nuts, seeds, and the intact cells in fruits and vegetables, provide substantial amounts of healthier, partially fermentable fibers which satisfy and feed our gut bacteria, support our gut cell walls, eliminate waste and harmful estrogens out of our bodies, and can even directly feed our colon cells that are a significant source of butyrate, able to reverse the extent of metabolic syndrome, among innumerable other health benefits.

CHAPTER 12

The Influence of Salt on Health

Sodium salts are inexpensive and unique in the range of flavors and mouth-feels they confer. They increase the superficial mouth-feel of food and thicken flavors, effectively increasing the synergy of food-flavoring systems. They are essential ingredients to the production of a wide range of convenience foods, can mask undesirable flavors (e.g. bitterness), and also help to intensify desirable flavors. In the case of sweet, salt directly stimulates sugar-receptor taste sensitivity. Salt added to protein can significantly increase human appetite and reduce the level of negative mood-elevating effects. It is widely used in other aspects of the food supply chain, such as to disburse liquids evenly for production processes that benefit from such a material property. Kreuter, spreading aids the meat during the manufacturing of sausages, improving both production efficiency and the quality of the final product. Therefore, excessive salt consumption is often described as a "downstream" effect of an ultra-processed diet.

The previous two examples illustrate how the consumption of salty foods contributes substantially to the total level of salt intake. Both of these examples also suggest guidelines to help promote reduction of salt intake. The guideline from the first example includes screens at non-food locations such as airports, bus stations, etc. In the second example, we recommend the labeling of the accurate and readily understandable sodium content of all processed and prepared food. Excessive intake of salt seems to be an inevitable accompaniment of consuming an ultra-processed diet.

CHAPTER 13

The Truth About Sugar and Sweeteners

The relationship between sugar and human beings is so ancient that it dictates, it is also problematic: the whole saga of slavery in the New World served to acquire a spice and medicine capable of giving immediate energy and making – in addition to cocoa and tobacco – the human being infallibly dependent. The easing of artificial sweeteners was invented to break free from this dependence, but then it also became so popular that we can no longer think of living without them. And in reality, after much research on the matter, we feel reassured because all this desire for sweet, sugary taste makes sense. It is mandatory because sugar is the brain's highly appreciable raw material.

The sweetest truth about sweeteners is that they offer one of life's simple pleasures: the irresistible pleasure of sinking your teeth into something sweet, the rush of energy that comes with it, the memories from our early childhood, and the foods that our mothers handed us when we felt blue – a piece of candy, a cake, a brownie. Surely all of it is hardwired. The human brain is perfectly able to absorb sugary drinks; its glucose is the favorite energy of neurons. That's why we have the sweet tooth that we have with such passion.

CHAPTER 14

The Connection Between Nutrition and Weight Management

However, due to the expense, invasiveness, and the risk of complications with bariatric surgery, it is not an option for most people who are significantly overweight. There must be a simpler way to accomplish this goal of healthy body weight. Our bodies' inborn regulatory system, the system that controls calories taken in and energy expended, tends to protect our current body weight. For most people only a small disturbance in this balance can lead to becoming overweight. Once weight is gained, it is hard to take off for two simple scientific reasons having to do with calories and weight set point. A simple approach to a complex issue, eating with portion control, is key to the goal of maintaining a healthy body weight. And when you need a simple food concept to focus on, remember this: if it comes in a box or a bag, it is not a single ingredient food.

Blame it on the "all-you-can-eat" buffet or our hectic lifestyle that promotes eating on the run, but it is estimated that over 60% of Americans are overweight and are not able to lose weight by dieting alone. We know that the first step to a healthy body is a healthy weight, yet obesity is on the rise. Because of the connection between obesity and the dramatic rise in the occurrence of diabetes, combined with a general recognition of how important it is to stay in shape, the World Health Organization now refers to it as "a public health crisis with worldwide epidemic distribution." And in a world-famous hospital, surgical procedures that have been developed to address this obesity issue are done on the human digestive system. The primary purpose of these invasive surgeries is to produce weight loss so that the individual can accomplish the holy grail of finding the perfect body with ease.

CHAPTER 15

The Impact of Nutrition on Mental Health

Eating very specific forms, vitamins, minerals, and other types of fiber that help our body to work can play an even more important role in all psychological health, when and if we also eat chemicals that can damage it. As mentioned in chapter 2, the gastrointestinal micro-organism-rich environment includes a variety of nutrients, including vitamins, in the form of minerals, and many other molecules related to the body to carry out operate normally. In the prevalence of aggressive and inflammatory lifestyles in modern times, there is still a wealth of seamless gaps to the inflammatory platform that provides a nutritious and healthful nutrition, which eventually stabilizes the neighboring masses and harms the tissues. Brain by brain, it causes physiological and biochemical changes that can affect neurons, stroma, and behavior. The dignity of nutrition claims that certain nutrition should increase the risk of developing neurodegenerative diseases. Consuming excessive obesity, trans fats, refined carbohydrates, starchy and homemaking products, etc., can cause metabolic overload affecting energy, hormone, neurotransmitter, brain inflammation, etc. Nevertheless, nutrition is more than as sole substance that causes risks. Compared to the reasonable dietary inputs that are carefully balanced because they are necessary for well-balanced activities, providing protection can provide therapeutic relief. In fact, one thing that is currently involved in the nutritional struggle of neuro-degeneration determines the long interference of alternative treatments along with energetic, especially fat, "physiologically active" procedures that are nominated as "exciting deals".

Food and psychological wellbeing are intertwined with each other. Although it is more complex than the old concept "tell me not only what you eat, but also how you lose yourself", the food we give to our lives also has a big impact on our head. Selecting some nutrients can help you manage yourself, and a healthier diet can significantly improve chromosomal symptoms and the quality of life. On the other hand, stress also affects our weight and often, especially our children with packages or candy, consumers are heard in the candy pocket. Unhealthy diet containing refined carbohydrates, sugar, fat, and salt may be directly attributed to the risk of the average distress and the mental state.

CHAPTER 16

The Importance of Gut Health

How does gut function address the twin aims of our working recipe? Firstly, ingestion and gentle early-stage digestion occur in our mouth and our upper stomach that lacked acidification at mealtimes. Meal breakdown in the upper stomach is an important aspect of why our primate kidneys are smaller than other similar-sized mammals, an adaptation that conserves lymph, urine, sugar, and protein for further use within how kidney function supports our plan for health. Sugar or glucose uptake from food is very important for our large brain but is not easily accomplished. Normally, sugar uptake into our proximal bowel is performed by our cells through the transport system regulated by the body's own produced components that are released to bind to at least four classes of sugars—glucose, galactose, sugar consisted of fructose— before being carted into our cells.

Our gut houses a population of beneficial bacteria, which collectively weigh more than the brain. This composition of microorganisms is known as our microbiome, and it is our most important organ of immunity and preferential gatekeeper of metabolism. Unfortunately, an unhealthy diet with wide-ranging consequences for our microbiome permeates much of the Western World, and the makeup of the microbiome is now understood to significantly influence the risk of many major age-associated conditions. Antiquity recognized the health benefits from ingesting fermented products such as yogurt, beer, and wine, which contain live organisms that sprout microbiome-boosting bioflora. This makes sense as warmer-climate hunter-gatherers can store food longer by fermentation than by any other method. Additionally, beneficial bacteria have yielded to new fermentable fibers and skin absorption of microbes, initiated by handling food coated in fertile organic soil, leading our immune system to improve.

CHAPTER 17

The Science of Food Allergies and Intolerances

One of the main issues in successful weight control is increasing insulin sensitivity and lowering insulin stress. Insulin sensitivity relates to how effectively body cells respond to insulin and take up glucose from the bloodstream: the more sensitive the cells, the easier it is to lose body fat, but the more resistant they are, the harder this becomes. Under stress, the body releases the hormone cortisol. Raised cortisol can also make weight loss significantly harder, particularly around the abdomen. A survey of 30,909 adults found the highest rates of obesity in those reporting the highest levels of perceived and chronic stress. Energy density and rapid carbohydrate absorption are known triggers of elevated insulin levels. Increased insulin concentrations are thought to exacerbate environmental and genetic factors and confer susceptibility to conditions such as obesity, insulin resistance, and hypertension.

Food allergies can be very serious, even life-threatening. However, food intolerances are much more common. Many people with food intolerances often do not believe that they could have a food allergy. As explained earlier, allostatic load, the cumulative wear and tear on the body from the initial reactions to socially or biologically significant stressors, activates the hypothalamic-pituitary-adrenal (HPA) axis and altered metabolic function. Stress and food intolerances can raise allostatic load. The regulation of the HPA axis involves cytokines, which are also central to the release of insulin during the regulation of metabolic stress.

CHAPTER 18

The Role of Nutrition in Aging Gracefully

Why do we age? The answer is not just the passing of time but the aging process that begins at birth. Sir , molecular biologist, Nobel Laureate, and Australian of the Year in 1960, said it best: "Death from malnutrition, infection, or trauma in the prime of life [almost never occurs]. In rich communities, death is very largely due to slow, pervasive, insidious change... which eventually makes an organ or system of the body inaccessible to life." Now, after moving through the 2000s, we know that degenerative and wasting diseases both come and go. Some of them even come and go twice. Age, the marker of those diseases, stays, and for our modern societies, age is going to be the trait that says the most about human biology and human history. Think about that the next time you think you are different from your neighbor, just because you speak a different language or carry a different 16th-century immigration card.

Living longer is high on the list for a great many people and in the future, we are likely to collect advice about living longer than Methuselah. To many, the quest seems beyond their control as if they are standing on the periphery with their hands tied. However, we have learned over the past decade that living longer is now a possibility and we can start today to make necessary changes in our lifestyles. Nutrient-rich foods, in right-sized portions, may both protect us against age-related diseases and help us to avoid obesity, the root cause of many life-limiting diseases. Just because we are aging does not mean that we must succumb to the conditions normally associated with the later years of life. Following good lifestyle choices can allow us to live illness-free and vigorous lives until the latter years of old age. We may not reach the ripe old ages of the scientists used in his experiments, then crossing the century threshold, but we should be able to reach the age where we can wear that tag of centenary with grace and joy, as Nobel Laureate has managed to do.

CHAPTER 19

The Link Between Nutrition and Chronic Diseases

As we have seen earlier in this book, cardiovascular diseases perhaps best demonstrate the powerful relation between adverse nutritional factors and chronic illness. Both large and small arterial vessels are subject to injury from increased concentrations of various substances in the blood. Hypertension has long been recognized as a feature of vascular injury. These injuries often occur coincidentally at the site of atherosclerotic plaques (the fatty deposits that are a hallmark of cholesterol-induced blood vessel disease) and thus are in large measure related to tissue oxygen requirements and availability. Atherosclerosis and its progression are the cornerstones of cardiovascular disease. Although plaque growth is slowly progressive, blockage of blood flow affecting the heart, the brain, or other organs, and more importantly in terms of sudden death, the destabilization of soft plaques causing arterial occlusion and ischemia, are much faster events.

Given the contributions of nutritional status to a variety of diseases, it is easy to see why the field of nutrition science, especially clinical nutrition, has burgeoned in recent years. Nutrition science and practice are aimed at minimizing vitamin and mineral deficiency diseases, obesity, diseases associated with the overconsumption of certain nutrients, and the lesser-known diseases that, because of their obscure relation to nutrition, have not yet been identified. If the current trends toward excessive consumption of energy-dense, protein-rich foods and reduction in physical activity continue, we can expect a pandemic of cardiovascular disease, diabetes, and possibly cancer in the decades to come.

CHAPTER 20

The Benefits of a Plant-Based Diet

The traditional Okinawan diet has been estimated to derive about 85% of its calories from sweet potatoes with a substantial amount of other vegetables and fruit. Which is why coherence means that it is the combination of foods that, when consumed in a particular way, appears to offer health advantages. Some of the studies carried out on the principles of coherence have led to a much better understanding of the effects of specific nutrients and phytochemicals. Of the many different nutrients needed that are derived from the human diet, some have more effects in common than others. For example, broccoli and curcumin have both been shown to have some beneficial health effects in human beings. Adding these effects together does not double the health benefits, but some of the effects are shared and so the combination can be very powerful.

Other components of the traditional Asian diet are vegetable-based soups, rice-based gruel, and many traditional fermented foods. The Japanese have over twenty words for seaweed and regional ferments of many different types. In Japan, kimchi is flavored with plums and rapeseed flowers in the Tokyo area but with chili in the Kyoto region. Traditional fermented foods also have probiotic activity, meaning that they contain live-friendly organisms. These have a beneficial effect on the host. These are foods made by natural fermentations with microorganisms that are part of a community living together. They actually promote the growth of a healthy cross-section of bacteria in the colon, which in turn draw out more nutrients from the food, benefiting the host.

CHAPTER 21

The Role of Probiotics and Prebiotics in Gut Health

Symbiotics are a combination of prebiotics and probiotics. There are a number of challenges that face the development of a new generation probiotic. The major challenge remains the survival of the probiotic through the manufacturing process, storage, and finally, the gastrointestinal transit, where it is usually exposed to a hostile environment in the form of acid. The doses required for the probiotics mean that millions or billions of organisms need to actually survive that transit. However, the failure rate of cleaning processes for crops and of antibiotic therapy remains unknown. These challenges may be overcome by complementing conventional probiotics with prebiotics, which create a more favorable environment for the beneficial bacteria to survive and thrive.

Probiotics are live microorganisms in foods that have a beneficial effect on the host, providing either a structural or a functional effect. For example, they may assist with the production of mucin, which helps surround the mucus and acts as a barrier. An example is found in yogurts. Prebiotics, on the other hand, are non-digestible compounds that beneficially affect the host by stimulating the growth and/or activity of beneficial bacteria in the colon. Indigestible carbohydrates such as those found in chicory root, artichoke, oats, asparagus, leeks, onions, garlic, wheat (fructans), and baobab fruit have been recognized as having potential prebiotic effects. There is a lot of promise in using a combination of pre- and probiotics in terms of their role in improving gut barrier function.

CHAPTER 22

The Science of Nutritional Supplements

Significant individual variability is also observed between the responses of healthy people to identical doses of the same nutrient, as is illustrated by studies showing DIM absorption increases 2.5-3.5 times in people taking levothyroxine, the omega-3 EPA/DHA in fish oil supplements being variably converted to an estimated 10-40 percent of omega-3 alpha-linolenic acid, resulting in further tissue omega-3 alpha-linolenic acid accumulation as high as 30-50 percent of the total fats found in red blood cells, blood plasma, and breast cancer biopsies, and 20 percent estimated reductions in blood saturated fats after a minimum of three fish oil supplement capsules, 900 mg combined EPA and DHA daily for 12 weeks, and also being variably converted to omega-3 EPA and DHA. Estimating what works for an individual's body, and enabling individuals to adjust their nutrient intake before, or after known challenges reflect the well-established truth, that consuming all the nutrients at DRI levels, in the most healthful proportions, is as scientifically valid as consuming the best shoe to fit onto almost every foot in the population.

The degree of individual variation in nutritional needs has been comprehensively quantified in studies showing that as many as 30 percent of healthy adults eating self-chosen diets still consume diets deficient in various vitamins (e.g. 93 percent of adults in one Swiss study whose blood levels of vitamins D3, K, and E were tested; and 55 percent of adults in another Swiss study whose blood levels of several nutritional elements were tested), and adults with certain genotypes are reported to have 11 percent lower omega-3 EPA and 42 percent lower omega-3 DHA levels in their blood and tissues. Since some genetic variations predict increased absorptive and metabolic demands for various nutrients, future studies are likely to further expand understanding.

CHAPTER 23

Understanding Food Labels and Claims

The NLEA delineated strict guidelines for the terms low-fat, no-fat, reduced, and less, which are found on food labels. These must be defined and used as follows: To be labeled low fat, the food must contain 3 grams of fat or less in a serving. If the food contains 0.5 grams of fat or less in a serving, it is considered fat-free. Diets low in fat and high in fruits and vegetables may reduce the risk of cancers of the digestive system. For example, if the product is labeled reduced-fat, it must contain at least 25% less fat, per serving, than the regular product or its predecessor. For example, if the product is labeled with the term less-fat, it must contain 25% less fat than the average fat content of comparable foods.

Responsible health professionals, government agencies, some food companies, and consumer groups all advocate reading and understanding the nutrition information on food labels to make informed food choices and establish a healthy diet. In 1990, the Nutrition Labeling and Education Act (NLEA) mandated that nutrition labels be printed on most packaged foods so that consumers are provided with consistent information on nutrient content of food products. The NLEA specified the type of information that must appear, and its format. Despite the effort to educate the public on how to use the nutrition facts label effectively, most people do not use it. Public awareness is one thing, but public use is quite another. It is not enough just to put the label on packages. If it were used, it could be a critical tool in the battle against diet-related diseases.

CHAPTER 24

The Influence of Marketing on Food Choices

The little voice in your head says things like dairy for strong bones or serotonin-rich turkey induces relaxation and sleep. Giving some children a cash award transforms carrots into candy, but the potential reward has to be large enough to motivate them for the change. Changing behavior is complex. Rewards are counter-productive in other situations. If you try to motivate children to consume an aversive food such as Durian fruit by telling them that they will be rewarded if they eat it, it can lead to increased food rejection in the future. Earning a reward is encouraging, but it also directs the focus from the actual behavior, so food becomes less tasty. Furthermore, parenting style has been related to how many and what kinds of foods infants will consume, and ritual has a big influence on what kids eat in the United Kingdom. Scone means Monday, Tuesday means soup. Children at pressured meals took a longer time to eat, consumed less, and rated the meal as less pleasant, according to a study.

The topic of the next few chapters is nutrition, but first let us untangle where your ideas about food come from. A four-year-old is interviewing you because that child wants to know how you decide what is good to eat or bad to eat. How do you know that is a bad food? The child is asking because the child is curious and hungry. Think about how you answer, or how you answered. You have to translate that personal, emotional feeling you have about a food into some kind of rationale or reason; some kind of story that, yes, babies like broccoli. When children think about eating, they already want to do what others are doing, and there is an amazing amount of information in the world to tell us, and our parents and our teachers how good or bad a particular food is.

CHAPTER 25

The Role of Nutrition Education and Public Health

We as Americans have arrived at a point where we are food-obsessed. Millions of overweight citizens are forced to debate the value of a single grape and how it will affect the scale. Between this obsession with fad diets and the green wavelength of our politicians, many important nutrition issues go ignored. We do have good reason to worry. According to the American Dietetic Association, nearly 250,900 overweight men and women die of heart attack, stroke, diabetes, certain cancers, and other related complications annually in the United States. This new statistic, as dramatic as it is, does not surprise the medical community whose members have been trying to battle the nutrition crisis for years.

I have been in the field of nutrition for over twenty years and have never seen a nation as nutritionally illiterate as the United States. Lack of nutrition education costs Americans millions of dollars annually in healthcare and unnecessary sickness and premature death. It is important that we put our money where our mouth is and demand that nutrition education become an integral part of the education system at every level. Not a holiday, birthday, or other cultural or social anniversary goes by without the public being warned about the dangers of smoking by every type of media imaginable. Where is our passion for nutrition education? Yet we hear no horror stories about six-year-olds who can only eat French fries and who die before they reach twenty because of premature heart disease and diabetes.

CHAPTER 26

The Impact of Socioeconomic Factors on Nutrition

It is possible to improve health through changes in the lifestyle of the most disadvantaged populations. It could be achieved by implementing standards that would improve the parameters of specific dietary characteristics. For example, poverty alleviation through actions aimed at increasing the income of the poorest populations could, in addition to providing access to their rights and improving their general living conditions, improve the food security of a large number of poor families through better access to dietary circuits, and increase the purchasing power of families, through the promotion of high production zones, rebuilding social justice, and any form of social protection.

We have seen throughout this book that low dietary quality and malnutrition are not solely the result of unavailability of food, but can also result from excessive consumption of unhealthy food. Both situations might coexist in the same country. This means that countries should adopt different strategies to combat malnutrition, which will be more effective if they are based on action throughout the supply chain (production, transportation, transformation, and commercialization of food). On the contrary, interventions focusing on only one link in the supply chain (e.g. dietary supplementation, concentrated development programs on food production, the distribution of seeds or livestock, electrification solutions) fail to be effective. This results in the absence of an increase in agricultural productivity, which weakens nutrition gains and prevents the poorest sections of the population from having access to the necessary resources that would allow them to counteract cyclical food stress. The failed strategies also perpetuate the many access and utilization issues encountered by vulnerable or excluded populations.

CHAPTER 27

The Future of Nutrition and Longevity Research

It is admittedly somewhat of a stretch to appeal to the comforting thought of the United Nations General Assembly having that odd after-breakfast stomach rumble and stopping in mid-session to rub cranky eyes and consider the implications of Toynbee's point. What can be said (without royally stretching) is that one of the great potential contributions of technological development is that it has made it possible to reach for the V-2 starting point even through peer-to-peer cooperation, sufficiently enlightened taxation policies, and the targeting of the best of triumphs. Nonetheless, one final word of caution is in order. Of all possible permutations, none would be sadder than to have the Wall Street/Park Avenue lobby (Georges Perec named all inventories of all possible permutations in his Life: A User's Manual, so his Wall Street one got his window in the long the sequence of fizz) and the Nobel Prize Committee both discover the value of the V-2 long before the budget managers and policymakers of governments. Simply sticking with key findings of nature is the only hope humankind can afford.

The future of nutrition and longevity research. Stated so far, the argument may come across as exceedingly negative, with signs of doom and gloom looming on every horizon. Are there some points of light in the darkness? True, if we properly appreciate the potential that lies in the healthcare system, and, more generally, in the network formed by the biotechnology, pharmaceutical, and food industry stakeholders, quite a few synergies can be identified, and we would have a chance to steer closer to the V-2 destination. This is probably the most encouraging part of the story. However, there is a need for a plan, and not too much time to waste if we are to have a chance to make some progress before we find ourselves hitting the wall of the demographic problem. In a rare optimistic moment, the historian Arnold J. Toynbee went as far as to suggest that today's unparalleled level of communication technologies and global interconnectedness could work in favor of humanity, for once providing for a sustainable development of civil behavior on a global scale. Are we so motivated to do so?

Practical Tips for Healthy Eating

One size does not fit all! This value focuses on the four basic principles of the national public health nutrition policy adopted by the Ministry of Health in Israel, and which emphasize the case for producing a varied and balanced diet. As part of those principles, we recommend interest of people to keep the nutritional intake correct, identifying the importance of changing lifestyle for the population in favor of health. This means that just as man does not live by bread alone has many dietary priorities, and a diet that succeeds in preventing various chronic diseases is actually a diet rich in a variety of plant foods and poor in highly processed foods. Eat at least five servings of fruit and vegetables daily (the size of each portion is up to 100 grams). They are filled with fiber, antioxidants, and minerals. Enjoy seasonal products which can be bought fresh and split easily. Eating a variety of diverse plants as well as season-specific plants, benefits diversity in the diet and ultimately in improving the health benefits of the gut microbiota.

Eat regularly to keep your energy levels up, and so as not to become insanely hungry, which may lead to overeating. Try to plan your meals and snacks around common times of the day. A balanced daily plan might include eating breakfast before leaving the house, having a small snack in the mid-morning, eating lunch in the early afternoon, having a small snack in the late afternoon, having dinner in the early evening, and having a small snack later in the evening. Do not try to lose weight by skipping meals. It is important not to skip meals as doing so may lead to loss of vital nutrients and underconsumption of unhealthy foods. Try to eat three well-balanced meals (with foods from each of the five food groups) each day and make nutritious snacks part of your daily plan. It is more important to eat a variety of nutrient-dense foods than to focus too much on specific percentage distributions of fat, carbohydrate, and protein intake. Consider the various health benefits of different nutritional mixtures, such as those of the Mediterranean diet.

CHAPTER 29

Recipes for Nutritious and Delicious Meals

A bit of dealing with the tempeh aside, here comes recipes where the produce shine because they must. Try crispy fresh greens, slivers of sweet red onions, chewy dried tomatoes, and tangy homemade peps! The crusty grilled breads are layered with tomato. And, just-you-wait, mmm! Aquafaba-aioli infused with a little garlic and lemon or apple-cider vinegar. What's that? Peps? Aquafaba? You're still in the smoked tempeh/phili club; of course, I have some 'splainin' to do! Let's whiz and get away from that little woman in lace now. Don't glower at me! Here we go! (Omit for oil-free; instead, press tempeh slices into seasoned nutritional yeast.) Slice one 8-ounce package of tempeh into eight equally thin pieces. Create the marinade for the tempeh by barbeque sauce, maple syrup, liquid smoke, soy sauce, mustard, and garlic powder, the more smoky-spicy, the theme you have it!, and vice versa. In a baking dish, pour over tempeh slices. Marinade and cure both sides.

If you like your club sandwich a little more intense, hot, smoky, or spicy, hear this. This takes a bit of prep, especially if you want to make the tempeh, roasted veggies, and vegan mayo the same day. Fortunately, you can make everything the day or three before, so assembly's a snap if you're a planner like me. Since making the Sriracha tempeh and roasted veggies would take most weekday lunches right into the doldrums of your workday, maybe plan to have those completely done with your mere-mortal sandwiches, and then the Smoked Tempeh Club can be an indulgence for the weekend if you're only cooking during short bursts. (Which is where sandwich planning prevails!)

CHAPTER 30

Frequently Asked Questions about Nutrition and Longevity

Is eating meat good for your health? Eating animal proteins in very small amounts is fine. We are not meant to be vegetarians and can handle a small amount of animal food, but ideally, twice a week at any mealtime is acceptable. Too much meat may contribute to chronic diseases such as cancer, heart disease, and diabetes. Ultimately, aim for most of your daily protein requirements to be fulfilled by completing the protein provided by grains and legumes or by combining dairy or egg products with a variety of plants at each meal.

What do you recommend as a general dietary guideline? Be a vegetarian - that is, someone who ensures that vegetables, fruits, legumes, and grains take up the majority of the space on their plate. Eat meat and fish as condiments in very small amounts. Do not rely on supplements to cover your dietary inadequacies because making wise food choices is the better route for optimal health and disease prevention. In the long run, eating poor quality nutrition will not fix itself with artificial supplements because these do not mimic the synergy generated by whole food. Hence, you need the variety of nutrients in plant foods to function optimally. Furthermore, whole foods contain so many other protective substances beyond the vitamins and minerals they provide.

Additional Resources for Further Reading

Nutrition and Health. These books are a mix of history and advice. By including a few older books, this list gives you a flavor of the long-term perspective. The dates are publication dates (and not, in some cases, the authors' death dates). And despite common use of quotation marks, the book titles were creative genius at work. Most of the titles from this early time period are in the public domain, so I was able to create free e-books for Kindle and e-pub readers that I have features on my author's website. You can also get these books at a fraction of what the commercially published books would cost. Basic advice hasn't changed much for the older books, but if you are interested in health or eating well, it's fascinating to go back in time and view the origins of nutrition advice firsthand.

In addition to Eat Smart, many excellent books and websites are available to help educate you about nutrition and health. I read extensively and even found old nutrition books helpful because they provided the long-term perspective that critics say is often missing from today's nutrition advice. The following lists provide some of the best books organized by topic. In addition to the books that are referenced throughout this book, they are all sources that I found helpful in writing Eat Smart.

Conclusion

In my lifetime, the United States has seen two major revolutions concerning nutrition. In the early 1900s, commodities such as sugar were sold without nutrition information and without ingredient lists. There was a fight by parent organizations to require the nutrition information to be provided, a fight which took the lifetime of a woman. Once we knew the calories from the food we eat, psychiatrists started looking for the cause of fatness in the heads of individuals. Along the way, health reformers Nathan Pritikin, his nutritionist Mary Corry, and Nathan's mother Rose proved over and over again to different individuals and even to different classes of students, at one time the equality of pigs purchased for consumption, that it was possible for average Americans to reduce hypertension and fatness and to improve heart disease risk factors by making intelligent selections. Based on their experiences, in 1980, they published the book "Eat More, Weigh Less" to describe the food components of the diet and how they achieved these results.

I hope my readers have gained a better understanding of the science of nutrition and longevity. Have you increased your understanding that the smarter we are in making decisions for handling the situations we face, the better are the chances we make decisions that help us in achieving what we desire? In health, the better we understand the factors that help or hinder our body in achieving its goals, the better

are the decisions we can make to help it. Have I been convincing or is it just wishful thinking? Have scientists reached a consensus about nutrition for health? I have read thousands of science papers and word is definitely a very long way off. It is extremely unlikely that all scientists will come to a consensus on the science of nutrition, and since money and health are at stake and conflicting information is presented by those seeking to market their food and gain customers, it is unlikely that news commentators will do so either.